When Mount Vesuvius erupted in Pompeii, human bodies left shapes in the ash, from which plaster casts have been made.

- **30BCE** The Ancient Egyptian Queen Cleopatra dies.

- **2CE** The world's first recorded census is held in China.

- **79CE** Mount Vesuvius erupts, burying the city of Pompeii in Italy.

- **c. 100CE** Indian mathematicians invent a number system like the one we use today.

- **c. 104CE** Paper is invented by T'sai Lun in China.

- **122–128CE** Hadrian's wall is built in Roman Britain and the Roman Empire is at its greatest extent.

- **c. 312CE** Roman Emperor Constantine converts to Christianity.

- **537CE** Hagia Sophia is completed in Constantinople (modern-day Istanbul, Turkey).

- **c. 552CE** Byzantine Emperor Justinian introduces silk production in Europe after smuggling silk worms out of China.

- **600CE** The Maya civilization in Central America is at its height.

- **618CE** The Tang Dynasty is established in China.

- **634–712CE** Muslim Arabs conquer the Middle East, North Africa, and Spain.

Chinese art and culture flourished during the Tang Dynasty.

The astrolabe was used in the Islamic world for navigation.

- **c. 800CE** Arab navigators perfect the astrolabe, used to predict the positions of the Sun, Moon, and planets.

- **c. 811CE** Paper money is first used in China.

- **868CE** The Diamond Sutra is printed in China. It is the world's oldest surviving printed book.

- **c. 872CE** The Vikings discover Iceland.

- **c. 900CE** The first castles are built in western Europe.

- **907CE** Collapse of the Tang Dynasty creates disagreement in China.

- **c. 1,000CE** Leif Erikson sails to North America.

100CE

600CE

900CE

Continued at the back of the book

A STREET THROUGH TIME

ILLUSTRATED BY STEVE NOON

CONTENTS

Penguin Random House

REVISED EDITION
Senior Art Editor and Jacket Designer Fiona Macdonald
Editorial Assistant Katie Lawrence

Design Assistant Katherine Marriott
Jacket Co-ordinator Issy Walsh
Managing Editor Laura Gilbert
Managing Art Editor Diane Peyton Jones
Senior Producer, Pre-Production Nikoleta Parasaki

Senior Producer Ena Matagic
Creative Director Helen Senior
Publishing Director Sarah Larter

Historical Consultant Dr. Stephen Haddelsey
Futurist Consultant Richard Watson

PREVIOUS EDITIONS
Editorial team Shaila Awan, Matilda Gollon, Dawn Sirett
Design team Sudakshina Basu, Sheila Collins, Shipra Jain,
Neha Sharma, Balwant Singh, Arunesh Talapatra, Anita Yadav
Managing Editor Linda Esposito
Managing Art Editors Peter Bailey,
C. David Gillingwater, Diane Peyton Jones

Publishing Director Jonathan Metcalf
Art Director Phil Ormerod

This edition published in 2020
First published in Great Britain in 1998 by
Dorling Kindersley Limited
80 Strand, London, WC2R 0RL

Copyright © 1998, 2012, 2020
Dorling Kindersley Limited
A Penguin Random House Company
10 9 8 7 6 5 4 3 2 1
001–316565–Jan/2020

A CIP catalogue record for this book is
available from the British Library.
ISBN: 978-0-2414-1154-4

Printed and bound in China

A WORLD OF IDEAS:
SEE ALL THERE IS TO KNOW

www.dk.com

THE STORY OF A STREET

Some streets and even some whole towns are very new. But there are some that are very old. Come with us and explore an old, old street. You will see how it has changed from a camp of nomadic hunter-gatherers, into a settled village, then a town, and then a city. Its progress has by no means been smooth! Sometimes the people living there have enjoyed peace and prosperity. At other times, they have faced war, sickness, and poverty. Some buildings in the street have survived, while others have been rebuilt many, many times. You'll also find out how people's way of life and standard of living have changed – not always for the better!

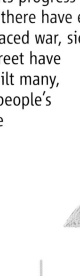

A RIVERSIDE SETTLEMENT

The river is central to the story of our street. Some 12,000 years ago it drew Stone Age hunters, pleased to have a good water supply and a handy source of fish! About 4,000 years ago, when farming had replaced hunting as a way of life, the river provided water for people, animals, and crops.

Later, the river brought trade to the village, helping it to grow and prosper. But the river sometimes brought troubles, too, such as invaders and disease. You can trace the changing role of the river as the story of the street unfolds.

CHANGING TIMES

For hundreds of years people farmed and lived in the village by the river. They slowly began to cut down the trees that covered the land, using them for fuel, to make tools and weapons, and as building materials. People's lives changed only slowly until the arrival of the Romans caused a total upheaval!

By about 100CE the village had become a wealthy Roman town. The local people lived in small flats and traditional huts, while the Romans occupied villas and large houses. Everything changed again when Rome's empire was invaded by barbarians. The town was destroyed and became part of a small village. People's standard of living dropped and the struggle to survive and prosper began anew. But it was to be shattered again, this time by Vikings in 900CE.

FROM VILLAGE TO CITY

Eventually the warlike Vikings began to settle and live with the people they'd once attacked. Traders who now sailed up the river helped the village to grow into a town. By the late 1600s the town had survived plagues and wars, but the real changes came in the late 1700s and early 1800s. Improvements in farming methods meant more people could be fed by fewer farmers on less land. Inventions brought the Industrial Revolution to our street, which was now in a growing city. There were new methods of transport, new industries, and new wealth. However, for some, life became even harder.

THE STREET TODAY

Our street remains in a city that has survived wars and spread so far that all the old forests and farmland have disappeared. The pace of change has become so rapid that people who lived in our street only 150 years ago would not recognize the modern businesses along the riverbank. People are much better off now than their ancestors.

STREET OF THE FUTURE

We cannot accurately predict what will happen in the future. But with help from children like you, we have been able to imagine what our street might look like in 50 years time.

STONE AGE (10,000BCE)

Once upon a time, everyone lived by hunting, fishing, and gathering food. People were nomads, moving across the land in small groups seeking food and shelter. This tribe has just found a place to spend the winter. The camp is the start of our street.

❶ The tribe's priest is calling on the spirit of the forest to bless the new camp under a deer skull – a symbol of the woodland god.

❷ The women use digging sticks to help them gather berries, nuts, and roots.

❸ Fish are caught with a net. Can you count how many fish have been caught already?

❹ Dogs are the only animals that people have tamed. Find the dogs fighting over food scraps.

5 Animal hide tent

5 Making a fire

Plucking a duck

Making a canoe out of a log

6 Cutting meat

7 Flint worker

Hunters

8

❺ The animals' meat is eaten, their fur and hides make clothes and tents, and their bones make tools.

❻ Some of the meat is dried and stored, ready for the winter months.

❼ Tools and weapons are made of flint, a type of stone.

❽ Forest stretches across the land and there are very few people. The next tribe is 50 miles (80 km) away.

FIRST FARMERS (2,000BCE)

More than eight thousand years have passed and people have learned
how to grow crops and keep animals. They have also developed new
skills, such as pottery making, weaving cloth, and metalworking.
The site by the river now has a permanent settlement with huts.

Stone circle

Using a bow
and arrow

Thatched
wooden hut

Palisade

Hunter

Pottery
kiln

Threshing

Winnowing   Spinning   Weaving   Sewing

Wolf

Harpooning
fish

❶ These people are using river clay
to make pots for the settlement.

❷ Fire is a great danger in wooden huts
with thatched roofs. It can spread quickly.

❸ The people have started to keep cattle,
pigs, sheep, and goats for meat and milk.

❹ Clothes are now made from woollen cloth as well
as leather and fur. The women spin, weave, and sew.

8 Barrow

7 Cutting crops

Cutting firewood

Blacksmith

Making a basket

Metal mould

Making flint tools

Roasting meat

Grinding wheat

6

5 Several villages have joined together to build a stone circle to honour the gods. How many stones are there?

6 A wooden palisade around the village protects the people from wild animals.

7 Wheat and barley grow in the field. The crops are cut with a sickle made from a sharp piece of flint.

8 Village dead are buried in a barrow, which is a grave covered by a mound of earth.

IRON AGE (600BCE)

Hundreds of years pass. People have now found out how to smelt iron to make better tools and weapons. The village has prospered, but there are battles with neighbouring tribes, who are fierce rivals.

Ancient stone circle

Sacred grove

Enemy heads

Cattle

Rival warriors

Thatched wooden hut

Food hut

Palisade

Loom

Pottery kiln ❶

Foreign trader ❷

Tattooing

Fishing

Wooden boat

6

❶ The potter has built his kiln away from his house because of the fire risk.

❷ This is a foreign trader. He has sailed up the river. The villagers are eager to buy his wine, silverware, and pots.

❸ These three wooden statues have been set up to honour the gods.

❹ Priests offer captured enemy weapons to the gods by throwing them into the river.

⑤ The chief has built a stronghold, called a fort, on the hill. It is made of wood. Spot two other monuments in the hills from earlier times.

⑥ After the warriors and the priests, the blacksmith is the most important man.

⑦ Little boats called coracles are made out of sticks and animal skin.

⑧ To help people farm, a more efficient plough has been invented with an iron ploughshare.

7

ROMAN TIMES (100CE)

The Roman Empire has spread across much of Europe, bringing a new way of life. Our village has become a town with hundreds of people. The town has large stone buildings, and a bridge has been built across the river for the first time.

Statue of Jupiter

Temple

Ancient stone circle

Small flat

Carpenters

Wall paintings

School

Bedroom

Domus

Bedroom

Barber's shop

Pottery shop

Tavern

Toilet

Kitchen

Baker's shop

Slaves

Local hunter

Wooden bridge

Atrium

Stove

❶ Most hard work is done by enslaved people. Here's a group of slaves arriving in the town.

❷ Most people go to the tavern for hot food because they live in small flats that do not have kitchens.

❸ A rich family lives in a town house, called a domus. The domus has beautiful statues and paintings.

❹ Some of the inhabitants of the old village still live in their huts. How many huts can you see?

Thatched huts

Basilica

Crane

Fountain

Fort

❺

Roman soldiers

Bathhouse

❻

Amphitheatre

❽

Wine warehouse

Pulley

Brick building

Imported wine in amphorae

❼

Merchant ship

❹

❺ The fort is where Roman soldiers are stationed. They do drills and marches, so they are always ready for action.

❻ People use the luxurious bathhouse to bathe or just to relax.

❼ Merchant ships bring goods such as wine, from all over the Empire.

❽ In the amphitheatre, gladiators often fight to the death to amuse the crowd.

THE INVADERS (600CE)

Barbarians have swept across Europe, destroying the Roman way of life. A group have settled in the ruins of our town. All the Roman comforts, such as baths and piped water, have been forgotten.

Ancient stone circle

Wolves

Columns from Roman temple

Shepherd boy

❶ Sheep pen

Thatched wooden hut

Chief

Weaving

❸

❷ Laying fish traps

❹

Wooden boat

❶ Sticks are used to make wooden fences. This stops the sheep from straying.

❷ The fish traps will help provide the villagers with extra fresh food.

❸ The chief and his son have been out hunting. The wild boar they have killed will be a welcome addition to the food stores.

❹ The Roman toilets have been destroyed!

Roman fort

Ancient barrow

Roman amphitheatre

Chief's hut

Food stores

Beggars

Blacksmith

Dried meat

Slave woman

Carpenter

Vegetable patch

Washing clothes

Coracle

❺ Wolves have taken a sheep. The shepherd boy tries to drive them away with his sling.

❻ The simple huts are made of wood. The chief has the biggest hut.

❼ This woman has found a strange shield in the river. Do you remember when it was used?

❽ Wood is used for cooking, heating, and building. Find three other people chopping or gathering wood.

VIKING RAIDERS (900CE)

The barbarians have now been settled for hundreds of years. They have become Christians and have grown prosperous. They have a king who gives his orders through the local chiefs. Now a new danger has appeared – fierce Viking raiders seeking treasure and slaves.

Ancient stone circl[e]

Stone church

Graveyard

Hole for smoke

Toilet

Viking longship

Viking

❶ The people flee. Women and children will be taken and sold as slaves.

❷ The village has some outdoor toilets. A very awkward place to be caught in a raid!

❸ Two boatloads of Vikings have rowed quietly up the river before dawn and taken the villagers by surprise.

❹ The church has gold and silver ornaments that attract raiders, but its books are likely to be burned.

Site of ancient Roman fort

Ancient barrow

Chief's hall with wooden roof

Thatched wooden hut

Sail rolled up

❼

Jetty

❽

❺ Unlike the huts, the church is built of stone and will not burn easily.

❻ An iron cooking pot can be a good weapon! This family may just be able to escape.

❼ Here's a person hiding in a barrel. Can you spot another under a table, and another under a basket?

❽ The villagers are in a panic. Some try to hide their treasure.

MEDIEVAL VILLAGE (1200s)

More than three hundred years have passed. The king has given the land to a lord, who has built a castle to protect the people from Viking raiders. The lord uses mounted warriors, called knights, to race to trouble spots. In return, most people have had to give up much of their freedom.

Ancient stone circ

Common land

Spire

Fallow land (unplanted)

Glass windows (used by the church and rich only)

Church

Peasant's house

Cobbler's shop

Baker's shop

Reed cutter's boat

❶ Villagers use the common to graze sheep and cattle. Can you count how many animals there are here?

❷ A ball game with boys from the neighbouring village is turning into a rowdy riot!

❸ It is cheaper to bring goods by river and safer, too – there may be outlaws in the forest!

❹ Entertainers play music for the crowds in the marketplace. They are called minstrels.

Stone castle

Keep

Castle wall

❼

❽

Miller's house

Windmill on site of ancient barrow

Barley strips growing

❻

Wheat strips growing

Chimney

Knight's stone house

Timber-framed house

❹

Dentist

Inn

Milkmaid

Blacksmith

Foreign merchant

❺

Pedlar

Sailing boat

❺ Today is market day. Some people have come from other villages to buy and sell goods.

❻ The village has three fields. Each villager has strips of land in each field.

❼ The lord has built a stone castle. From it, he can control all the land around.

❽ Villagers grind their grain in the lord's mill. They think the miller keeps some of their flour! **15**

MEDIEVAL TOWN (1400s)

Thanks to the trade brought by boats up the river, the village has grown into a town. Its citizens have purchased a charter from their lord. This allows them to run the town. Some of the merchants have become very rich, and can afford to improve their houses and shops.

Church

Wine merchant's house

Collecting firewood

Bedroom

Doctor

Cobbler's shop

❶

Shutter

Weaver's shop

Baker's shop

Kitchen

Merchant lending money

Selling wine

Religious procession

Cellar

Stone bridge

❶ Household waste gets thrown into the street.

❷ In the bustling town, shopfronts are lowered and used as counters by the shopkeepers.

❸ Petty thieves are placed in the stocks, and the gibbet is used to hang murderers.

❹ Can you guess what the inn is called from the sign outside it?

Windmill

Miller's house

Turret

Stone castle

❻

Town
guard

Deer hunters

Gibbet

❸

Guildhall

Tapestry

Indoor
toilet

❼

Glass window

Market cross

❹

Inn

Armourer's workshop

❽

Stocks

Foreign
merchant's ship

Black rats come
off the ship

❺

Lord and his wife
return from a visit

❺ This man has found an ancient helmet.

❻ The lord is making improvements to his
castle to make it more comfortable.

❼ Rich citizens can afford to
have an indoor toilet, of a sort!

❽ Craftsmen have formed guilds. These unions
protect the craftsmen and set standards of work. **17**

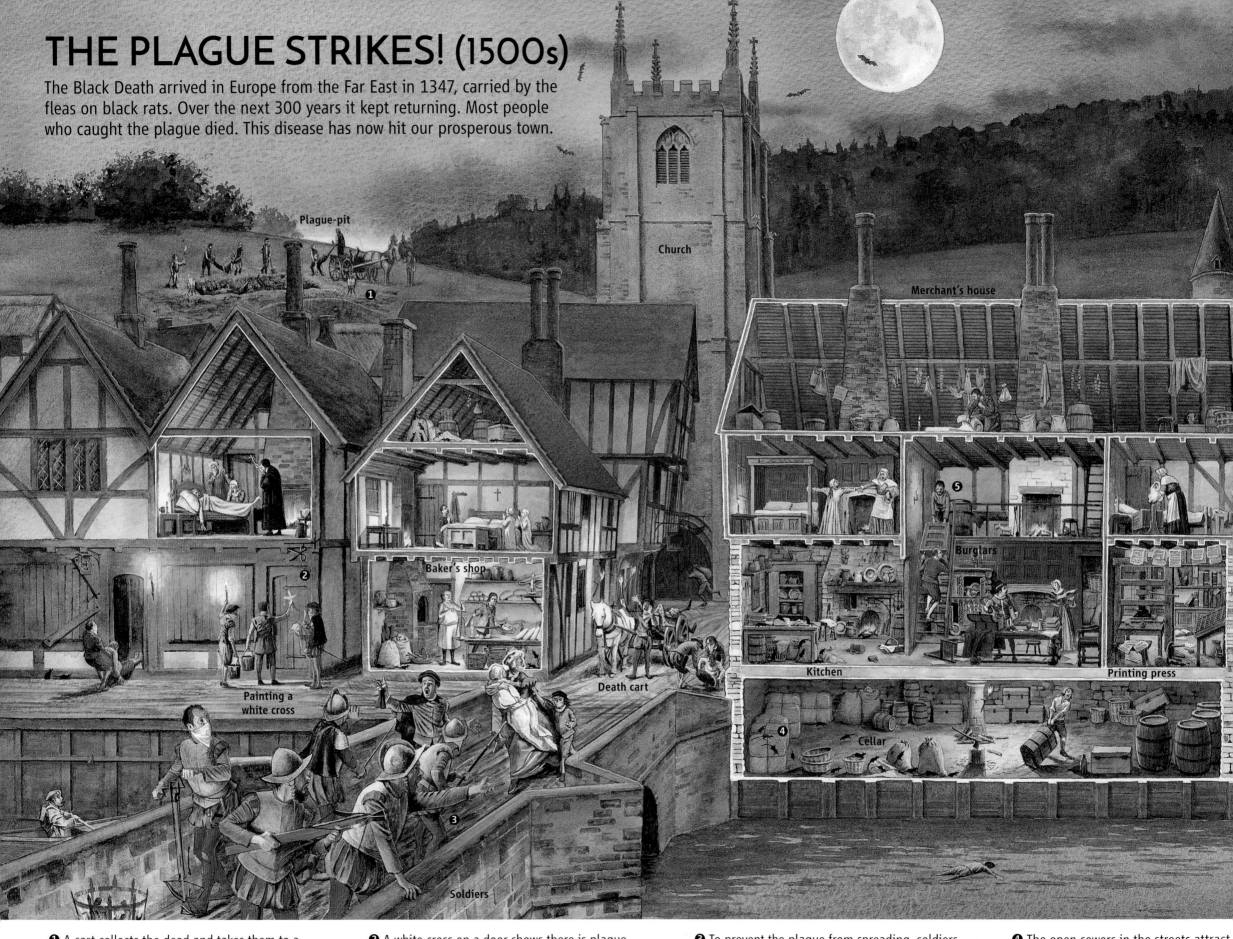

THE PLAGUE STRIKES! (1500s)

The Black Death arrived in Europe from the Far East in 1347, carried by the fleas on black rats. Over the next 300 years it kept returning. Most people who caught the plague died. This disease has now hit our prosperous town.

Plague-pit

Church

Merchant's house

Baker's shop

Burglars

Printing press

Painting a white cross

Death cart

Kitchen

Cellar

Soldiers

❶ A cart collects the dead and takes them to a plague-pit where the bodies are buried together.

❷ A white cross on a door shows there is plague inside. How many other doors have white crosses?

❸ To prevent the plague from spreading, soldiers have been sent to stop people from leaving town.

❹ The open sewers in the streets attract the rats. They are everywhere now!

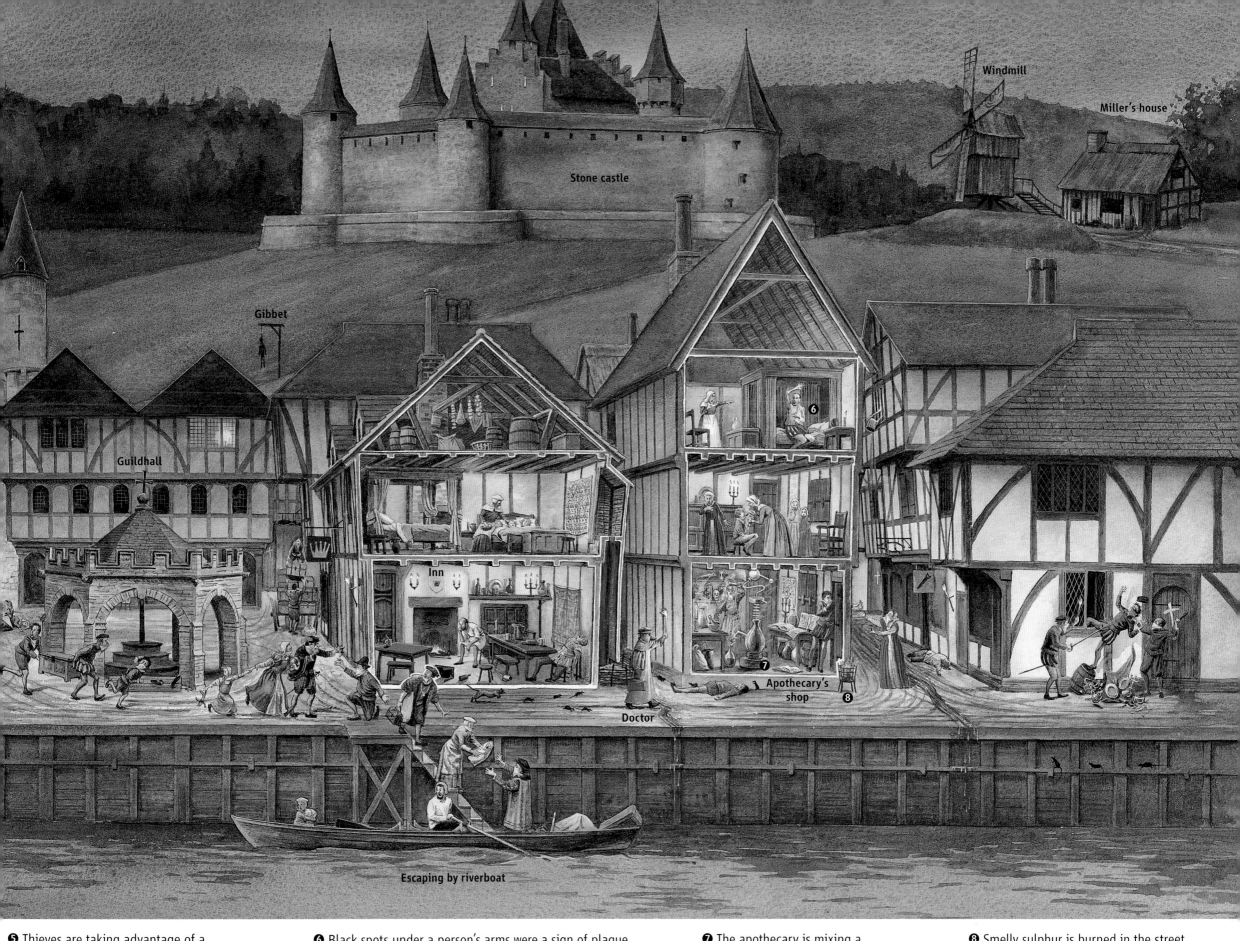

Windmill

Miller's house

Stone castle

Gibbet

Guildhall

Inn

Doctor

Apothecary's shop

❻

❼

❽

Escaping by riverboat

❺ Thieves are taking advantage of a family's illness by stealing their valuables.

❻ Black spots under a person's arms were a sign of plague.

❼ The apothecary is mixing a potion to find a cure for the plague.

❽ Smelly sulphur is burned in the street to try to get rid of the deadly infection.

UNDER ATTACK! (1600s)

War has broken out. The people are fighting over religion and about who should rule the country. The castle and town are both under attack, and the townspeople are losing! Not even the castle walls can withstand the pounding of the improved cannons.

Church

❶ **Enemy soldiers**

❷

Cobbler's shop

Tailor's shop

Town soldiers

Kitchen

Merchant's house

Printing press

❸

20 ❶ Enemy soldiers have broken into the town, killing, destroying, and stealing.

❷ Some people climb on to the roof of their house, hoping they can escape from the enemy.

❸ People are in a panic. Some try to hide their valuables, others try to escape with them.

❹ Guns, called muskets, are in use. They fire only one bullet, then have to be reloaded.

Windmill

Miller's house

Stone castle

Doctor

Stone house

Inn

Cannon

❺ Cannons have been around a long time, but the new ones are more powerful. How many buildings have been set on fire by cannonballs?

❻ Two people are hiding under a bed from an enemy soldier.

❼ The innkeeper is being threatened with a pike, a nasty weapon carried by foot soldiers.

❽ Anaesthetics do not exist, but the doctor has to cut off a patient's shattered leg.

AN AGE OF ELEGANCE (1700s)

Peace has returned and the town is prospering again. Some houses have been repaired, while others have been rebuilt in the latest style. The wealthy citizens have a lot of spare time. They pride themselves on their polite manners, their learning, and their elegant parties.

❶ Wigs are very fashionable now. This man is choosing a new one.

❷ Plaster and colourful wallpaper have replaced the old wooden panelling inside the houses.

❸ The new lord has left the ruined castle and now lives in a beautiful mansion.

❹ Sedan chairs are hired by wealthy people so that they can travel in comfort through the streets.

❺ A mailcoach speeds out of the inn. These coaches carry passengers as well as mail from town to town.

❻ These people have found a treasure chest. When was it buried?

❼ Recently, coffee has been imported and has become a fashionable drink.

❽ Some people sell fruit, flowers, and other goods in the busy street.

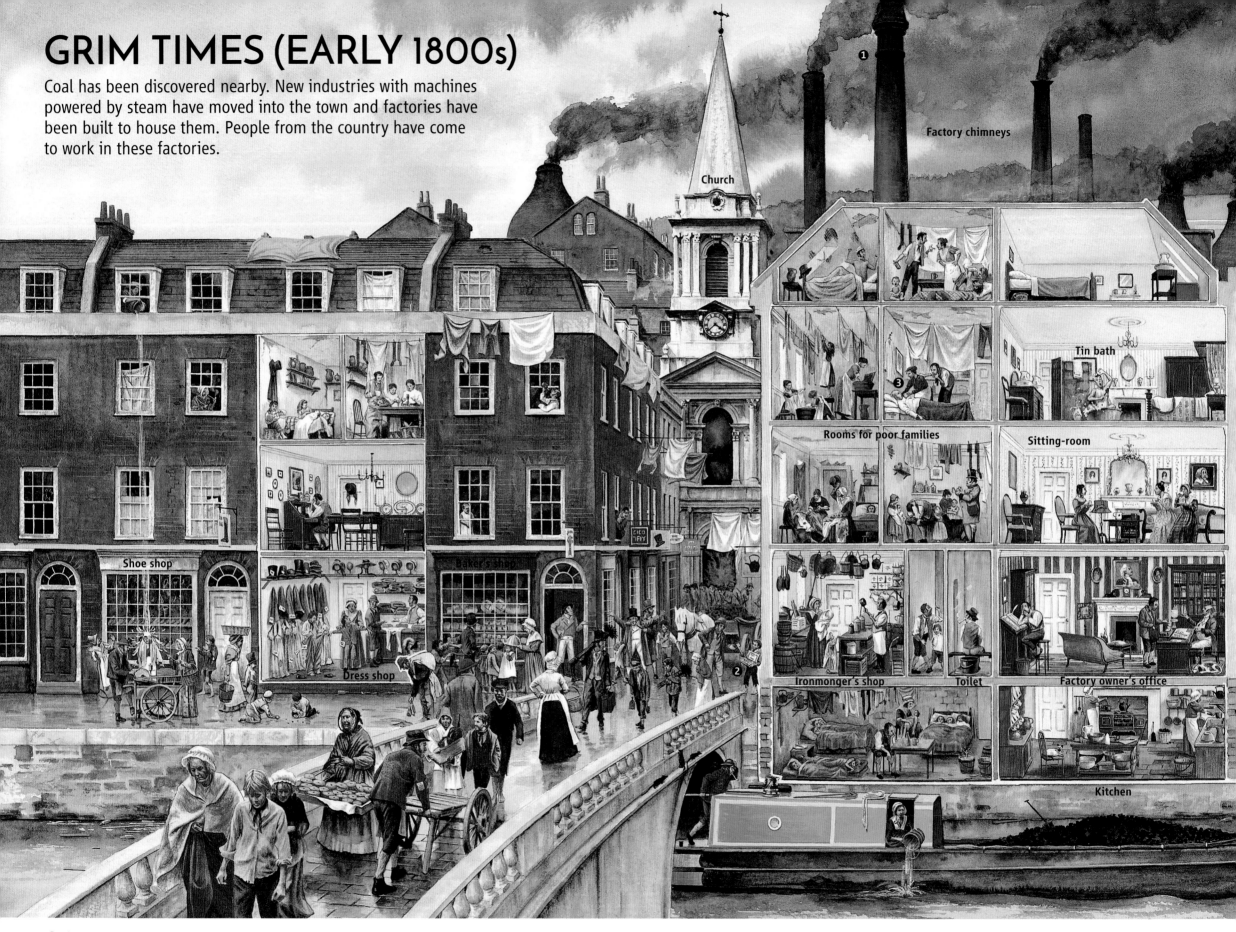

GRIM TIMES (EARLY 1800s)

Coal has been discovered nearby. New industries with machines powered by steam have moved into the town and factories have been built to house them. People from the country have come to work in these factories.

Factory chimneys

Church

Tin bath

Rooms for poor families

Sitting-room

Shoe shop

Baker's shop

Dress shop

Ironmonger's shop

Toilet

Factory owner's office

Kitchen

❶ The air is now polluted by the smoke bellowing from all the factory chimneys. How many factory chimneys can you see?

❷ Poor children have to work too, so that they can earn money. Most cannot read or write.

❸ With the overcrowding, the dirt, and the polluted water many people become ill.

❹ A few brave men are experimenting with a new form of travel – a hot-air balloon.

24

5 Some people drink to forget their misery. This drunk is in danger of falling off the roof!

6 These men are using children to pick pockets for them.

7 Heavy goods, such as coal, are carried by barges. The barges are pulled along by horses on the riverbank.

8 There are no homes to look after orphans. Some live and sleep in the street.

FROM TOWN TO CITY (LATE 1800s)

Thanks to its industries, the town has grown into a city. Many people are better off, and working and living conditions have improved. A new railway line now begins in our street and carries people and goods to other towns or cities.

Church
Nursery
Bedroom
Bedroom
Bathroom
Lacing a corset
Railway station
Station restaurant
Master study
Sitting-room
Railway ticket office
Draper's shop
2
Steam engine
Postbox
3
1
Lamplighter
Stockroom
Kitchen

❶ Streets are lit by gas lamps. This man lights the street every evening.

❷ For the first time, people can travel long distances quickly and cheaply using the new railways.

❸ A cheap postal service has been set up. People post their letters in the postbox.

❹ Police now help to keep order and fight crime.

Growing suburbs

Castle ruins

Factory chimneys

Inventor

Town hall

Guest-room

Guest-room

Guest-room

Guest-room

Restaurant

Shoe shop

Omnibus

Public bar

Inn

Saloon bar

Toy shop

Road sweeper

Cellar

Photographer

Steam boat

❺ People can travel around the city cheaply using the horse-drawn omnibus. How many more can you see?

❻ People who have made their fortunes from factories have built houses away from the city centre.

❼ Steam engines are now used to power boats as well as locomotives.

❽ The photographer is about to take a picture of the men who are going to try out their new diving suits.

THE STREET TODAY

In recent years there has been much change in our city. Modern businesses have replaced most heavy industries, people have become more environmentally aware, and leisure time has increased for many people.

Helipad

Crane

Hospital

Flats

Hairdresser's shop

Artist's studio

Dentist

Bathroom

Lawyer's office

Church

Bookshop

Bank's office

Café

Museum

❶

Museum shop

Clothes shop

Bank

Gym

Safe

Jogger

Rowing boat

❷

❶ Trains no longer use the railway station. It is now a museum, housing objects from the past.

❷ Large passenger planes enable people to travel abroad easily and quickly.

❸ Men dredging the river have found a chest. Who dropped it and when?

❹ Inventions such as washing machines and vacuum cleaners make domestic work easier for everyone.

Castle ruins

Tourists

Town hall

Nursery

Bathroom

Sitting-room

Kitchen

Café

Shoe shop

Solar panels

Tram

Restaurant

Wine bar

Antique shop

Motor cruiser

Dredger

❺ There is a smart new town hall. Look how much glass has been used to build it!

❻ Many people who work in the city live in houses or flats that have been built around it.

❼ The castle is now a protected ancient monument and an important tourist attraction for the city.

❽ The city is starting to use renewable energy from this wind farm.

STREET OF THE FUTURE

In 50 years, our street might look something like this. Improved healthcare and worker robots mean that people both live longer and have even more leisure time. The population has increased, so there is a lack of space and architects have to be creative. Protecting the environment is challenging, but there are measures in place to help reduce pollution.

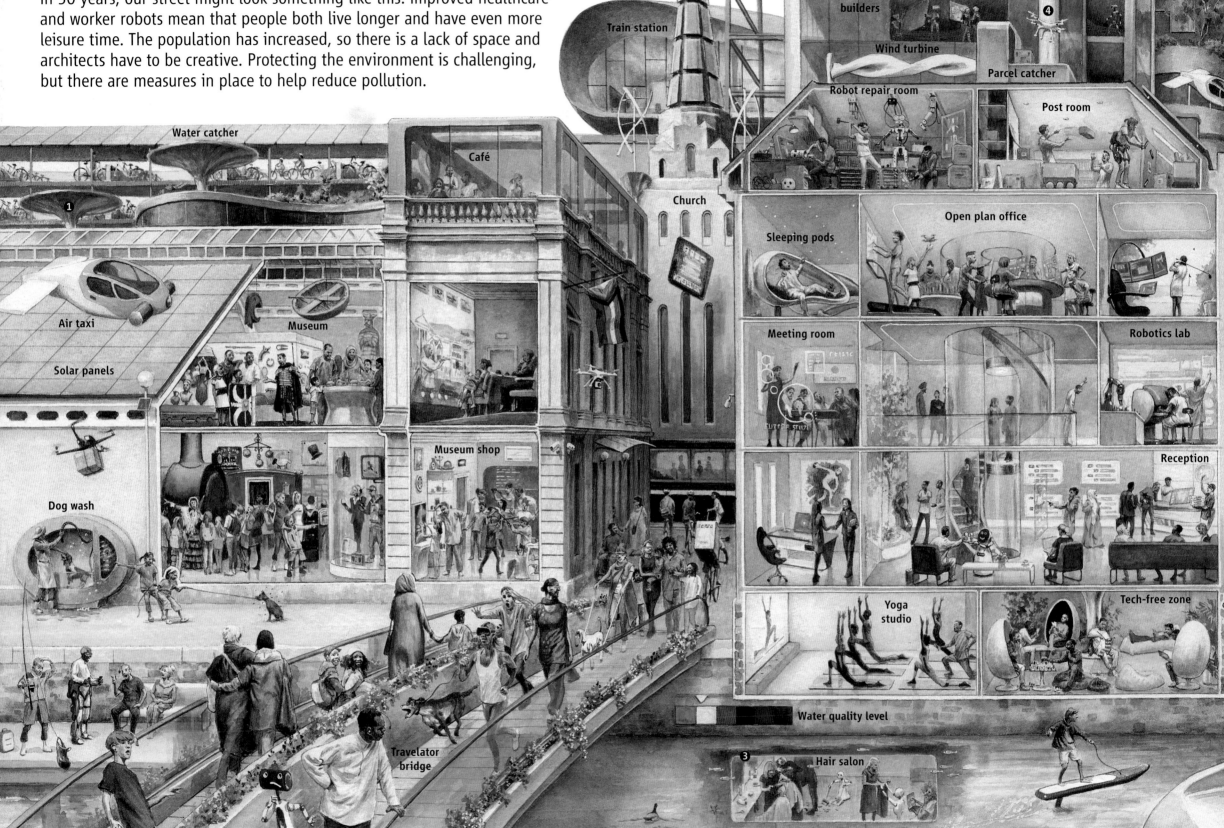

Train station

Robot builders

Wind turbine

Parcel catcher

Robot repair room

Post room

Water catcher

Café

Church

Sleeping pods

Open plan office

Air taxi

Museum

Meeting room

Robotics lab

Solar panels

Museum shop

Reception

Dog wash

Yoga studio

Tech-free zone

Water quality level

Travelator bridge

Hair salon

❶ Water catchers collect rainwater, which is recycled and used for washing, cleaning, and drinking. How many water catchers can you see?

❷ Space travel has become cheap and many people fly to space on rocket ships like this one.

❸ As well as building upwards, architects have started to make use of underwater space.

❹ Drones drop parcels into chutes on top of buildings.

Skyscraper farm ❼

Castle ruins

Recycling centre

...nd ...ines

Castle visitor centre

Zip line

Town hall

Maglev train ❻

Retirement home

Bedroom

Bathroom

3D printing scanner

...ppiness level ❺

Lounge and kitchen

Air pollution level

3D printing shop

Food hall

Insect café

Tram

Bar

Bookshop

Upcycling clothes shop ❽

Self-steering yacht

Electric bikes

Rowing boat

❺ The biggest circle on the happiness level shows how happy the people in our street are.

❻ People use maglev trains to travel long distances quickly.

❼ As the population has grown, there is less green space to farm on. This means that some farms are now on top of skyscrapers.

❽ People take their old clothes to upcycling shops to be made into new outfits.

GLOSSARY

amphitheatre
Oval or round building with seats. Used by Romans for wild beast shows and gladiator fights

amphorae
Clay jars with two handles. Used by Greeks and Romans to store wine and other liquids

anaesthetics
Medicine given to patients to stop them feeling pain during an operation

apothecary
Person who makes and sells medicine

architect
Person who designs buildings

atrium
Central courtyard in a Roman house with the rooms opening off it

barbarians
Romans referred to people who lived outside the Roman Empire as "barbarians". In particular, the word is often applied to people from north and northeastern Europe who began invading the Empire after 200CE

barrow
Old type of grave, consisting of an earth mound over burial chambers

basilica
Roman building. Law cases and other town functions were held here

BCE
Abbreviation used in dates. It stands for "Before the Common Era", which covers the period of history before Jesus Christ was believed to have been born

CE
Stands for the "Common Era", the period after the year Jesus Christ was believed to have been born

charter
Written document given by a king or a lord granting rights to someone

Cold War
Period of hostility that existed from 1945 to 1989 between the United States and the Soviet Union and its allies. It never resulted in violent warfare

coracle
Small oval boat made from woven sticks and covered by a waterproof material

crusader
Soldier who engages in a holy war

democracy
Government that is elected by the people

domus
Roman town house used by a wealthy family

drone
Type of flying machine that does not require a pilot. Someone on the ground controls it

dynasty
Line of rulers from the same family

empire
Large area, with different peoples, under the rule of a single powerful state or people

French Revolution
Period of great social and political upheaval in France, which saw the downfall of the French monarchy and aristocracy

gibbet
Wooden gallows where criminals were put to death by hanging

guildhall
Place where guild members met to run their guilds and the town

guilds
Unions of craftsmen or merchants that controlled working standards, conditions, and prices. They also cared for members in trouble

harpoon
Spearlike weapon used to kill prey

hieroglyphics
Ancient Egyptian writing system using picture symbols carved in stone

Industrial Revolution
Period during the 1700s and 1800s when there were huge changes in the way people lived and worked. This was brought about by new inventions that led to factories producing goods faster than people could at home

Iron Age
Although people were experimenting with iron by 1,100BCE, the period of history known as the Iron Age began about 900BCE, when iron replaced bronze for making tools and weapons

jetty
Landing place on a river or in a harbour

keep
Stone building that was the inner stronghold of a castle

longship
Viking warship with oars and a square sail

maglev train
Type of train that travels at high speeds. Magnets underneath the train propel it along the train track

nomads
People who wander from place to place seeking food and shelter

palisade
Fence of strong wooden poles built around a fort or village to help defend it from enemies and wild animals

patent
Document giving an inventor sole rights to an invention

pedlar
Travelling salesman

plough
Machine or tool used in farming to prepare the soil for sowing seeds

recycling
Process that turns used materials into new products

robotic
Relating to robots

Roman Empire
Around 200BCE, Rome began conquering other lands and created an empire that was to last in western Europe until 476CE. At its height, it covered much of Europe, North Africa, and parts of the Middle East

sickle
Handheld tool usually with a curved blade used to cut crops

sling
Piece of leather or woven material used to hurl stones

Spanish Reconquest
Period of almost 800 years during the Middle Ages when Christian kingdoms succeeded in retaking areas of Muslim-controlled Spain

stocks
Wooden frame with holes for feet, neck, and hands. It was used to punish small-time criminals

Stone Age
Period of history that lasted roughly 2.5 million years when tools and weapons were made mostly of stone. It began when the earliest people made their first tools and lasted until metal was introduced

suburb
Area on the outskirts of a city where people live

sulphur
Yellow substance that burns with a choking smoke and horrible smell

thatched roof
Roof made of straw

threshing
Beating a harvested cereal plant to separate the seeds

upcycling
Repairing or decorating something old such as an item of clothing to make it feel new and fashionable again

vaccine
Medicine, usually an injection, that stops the body from catching a disease

Vikings
Fierce warriors from Norway, Sweden, and Denmark. They raided and settled in parts of Europe between 790CE and 1100CE

winnowing
Tossing grains into the air to separate them from their light cases

INDEX

CREDITS

DK would like to thank: Abigail Luscombe and Seeta Parmar for proofreading, Claire Morrison for organising the Street of the Future competition, and Tom Morse for creative support.

The Publisher would like to thank all of the children and schools who sent in their futuristic ideas and drawings for the Street of the Future illustration competition.

The Publisher would like to thank the following for their kind permission to reproduce their photographs:

(Key: a-above; b-below/bottom; c-centre; f-far; l-left; r-right; t-top)

Endpaper images: *Front:* **Dorling Kindersley:** Ashmolean Museum, Oxford (cb); Museo Archeologico Nazionale di Napoli (c); National Maritime Museum, London (tr). **Dreamstime.com:** Lightfieldstudiosprod (tc); **Getty**

Images: De Agostini (tc, Romulus and Remus); Danita Delimont (bl). *Back:* **Corbis:** Bettmann (cb, tr); **Dorling Kindersley:** Bethany Dawn (tl); Musee du Louvre, Paris (tc); **NASA:** (br).

All other images © Dorling Kindersley

For further information see: www.dkimages.com

Angkor Wat in Cambodia is the largest temple complex in the world.

- **1180** Angkor Empire of Cambodia reaches its greatest size.

- **1187** Saladin, Sultan of Egypt and Syria, defeats crusaders and takes Jerusalem.

- **1206** The Mongol Empire is founded by Genghis Khan.

- **1215** The Magna Carta is signed, giving the English people certain rights.

- **1271** The European explorer Marco Polo travels to China.

- **around 1280** Polynesian people discover and settle in New Zealand.

1200s

- **1405–1433** The Chinese set out on seven major expeditions, travelling as far west as Africa.

- **1421** Beijing becomes the capital of the Ming Empire in China.

- **1453** Ottoman Turks capture Constantinople, ending the Byzantine Empire.

- **1455** The Gutenberg Bible is printed using the first modern printing press.

- **1492** Christopher Columbus lands in America.

- **1492** Spanish Christians retake the city of Granada from the Moors, completing the Spanish Reconquest.

Christopher Columbus sailed to America on the *Santa María*.

1400s

The *Mona Lisa* is one of the world's greatest masterpieces.

- **1503** Leonardo Da Vinci starts painting the *Mona Lisa*.

- **1509** Henry VIII becomes King of England.

- **1519–33** The Spanish conquer the Aztec and Inca empires.

- **around 1530** Beginning of the African slave trade from West Africa to European colonies in the New World.

- **1543** Astronomer Copernicus challenges the view that the Earth is at the centre of the Solar System.

- **1596** Englishman John Harington invents the flushing toilet.

1500s

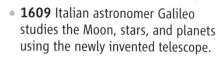

- **1609** Italian astronomer Galileo studies the Moon, stars, and planets using the newly invented telescope.

- **1620** Pilgrim fathers (early settlers) leave England and sail to live in America.

- **1642** The English Civil War breaks out.

- **1653** The Taj Mahal is completed in Agra, India.

- **1682** The Palace of Versailles is built near Paris, France, for the French king, Louis XIV.

- **1687** The scientist Isaac Newton publishes his theory of gravity.

With his telescope, Galileo spotted the four largest moons around Jupiter.

1600s